SAVAGE
SUNSETS

Other Works by Adrian C. Louis

Poetry:

The Indian Cheap Wine Séance (1974)

Muted War Drums (Chapbook, 1977)

Sweets for the Dancing Bears (Chapbook, 1979)

Fire Water World (1989, 2012)

Among the Dog Eaters (1992, 2012)

Days of Obsidian, Days of Grace (1994)

Blood Thirsty Savages (1994)

Vortex of Indian Fevers (1995)

Ceremonies of the Damned (1997)

Skull Dance (Chapbook, 1998)

Ancient Acid Flashes Back (2000)

Bone & Juice (2001)

Evil Corn (2004)

Deer Dreams (Chapbook, 2006)

Logorrhea (2006)

Archeology (Chapbook, 2011)

Savage Sunsets (2012)

Fiction:

Skins (1995, 2002)

Wild Indians & Other Creatures (1996)

Edited:

Shedding Skins: Four Sioux Poets (2008)

SAVAGE SUNSETS

Adrian C. Louis

West End Press
Albuquerque, New Mexico

Some of the poems in this collection, a few in earlier versions, were published previously in *The Nation, New Letters, North American Review, Café Review, Kenyon Review, Crazyhorse, Yellow Medicine Review, Superstition Review, Poets of the American West, Washington Square Review, Exquisite Corpse, Omega, Mandorla, Red Rock Review, SNReview, Chiron Review, Barn Owl Review, Spirit Magazine, The Ruined Place: Poems of Human Rights, Askew, Los Angeles Review, The Meadow, West Wind Review, Water-Stone Review, South Dakota Review, New Mexico Poetry Review, San Pedro River Review, Three Coyotes, Gargoyle Magazine, Mas Tequila Review, Willow Springs, Natural Bridge, New Madrid Journal, Seizure State, Sage Trails, Two Step: A Native American Anthology, La Llorona: An Anthology,* and *The Willow's Whisper: Irish & Native American Poetry.* "The End of The Trail Is A Beginning of The Trail" appeared as an introduction to *Shedding Skins: Four Sioux Poets* (Michigan State University Press). Other poems first appeared in *Archeology*, a chapbook published by Tavern Books.

Thanks and gratitude to the editors of the aforementioned publications. Thanks also to Sandy Mosch, Erzebet Yellowboy, David Pichaske, Paul Rowley, Sky Hopinka, Trevino Brings Plenty, and Susan Betz. Special thanks to John Crawford.

Saavage Sunsets © 2012 by Adrian C. Louis
Printed in the United States of America

First print edition September 2012
ISBN 978-0-9826968-7-3

WEST END PRESS
PO Box 27334 • Albuquerque, NM 87125
www.westendpress.org

Cover art by Dean Pasch
Book design by Bryce Milligan

for Colleen

Toksa ake...

The sun was like a great visiting presence that stimulated and took its due from all animal energy. When it flung wide its cloak and stepped down over the edge of the fields at evening, it left behind it a spent and exhausted world.

—WILLA CATHER

CONTENTS

SAVAGE SUNSETS

ARCHEOLOGY

We turned our backs & spit
out the medicine of salvation.
We let the sun melt us in a
sweet conspiracy of heat.

Liquefied, we seeped
under white, alkaline soil
& shrugged when wagon
train wheels rolled over us.
We arose, dusted ourselves
off, but we'd been mottled
& mutated. We spoke
a strange, new language
like mashed potatoes
with their skins left on.
We began to whisper
lies to our children &
they turned on us.

WABUSKA

Faded years ago
fat & sacred magpies
gnashed *yuwepooee* berries
on the shaded eastern end
of the buckbrush & I joined
them, toying with red fruit.
Sated, Messiah's birds fled
& I followed, my voracious
wings flinging me far from
my home of eighteen years.
I circled clouds for decades
until I fell to the dry bones
of the Dakotas & made from
memory, a replica of home.
I became a citizen of my heart
& turned as gray as the lie
that at any day I could scrape
all the asinine clichés & excuses
from my old tongue, cook them
down in a silver spoon, resurrect
my wings & magically flap back
to the ghost clouds of childhood.

for Sassy

Stereotypes

drug use

4

INDIAN THIGHS

Across the black belt
of night, star fires tease
faint memories of meat.
I cross the wide Missouri
into Indian territory where
years ago smoke blended
campfire shadows of women
into dappled trees of autumn.
Now, it all seems so contrived
& the essential fictive nature
of public utterance keeps me
from saying so much more.
This is no age to be a victim.
If the court of night compels
testimony, I will defer to
the dark claims of crickets
who remember better than
I, those searing flame songs
once fueled by Indian thighs.

HOUSE OF SPIRITS

In the Wal-Mart yesterday I saw
a dead person reading expiration
dates on packs of Hormel bologna.
I was standing right next to her,
but I quickly spun my head before
she could catch my eyes & make
me wander the aisles of eternity.
She was wearing a halter top.
Her back was blue & so was
the hungry sky I ran towards.
I scowled at the smiling sun,
searched my pockets frantically
for my keys, finally found them,
closed my eyes & drove fast
past the leering liquor store
& its septic, electric signage.

ROCKABILLY BLUES

Rock.
Rock.
Rockabilly, rock.
Really Billy, really, really rock.
Shake your silly hillbilly flock.
Sing the Pledge of Allegiance.
Sing all the dire anthems
of the coming apocalypse.
Sing the burning bush.
Sing the Wall St. blues
& bow down before
the bedonkadonk
of Britney or the Brits
at old Bunker Hill.
It's all good...
It's all Davy Crockett.

WHITE LIES

Silent as the valley snow, he hides
behind a pine, his bowstring taut,
the morning smell of his woman
still upon him, sunlight glinting off
the obsidian point hafted by pitch
& sinew to a tule shaft with feathers
of mallard, though he wants to think
hummingbird, wants his target to
feel the sharp, blurring beak like
a hypodermic into the eye which
would suck away all white lies.

Stereotypes formed by white aesthetic

COYOTE

The genesis of the creature
that crawled in from a cold
desert & did dogged tricks
for fat, naked hippies is almost
possible to discern now & again
with an application of strong spirits,
but the hole where his howling,
hilarious soul was ripped out
makes memory moot.

To go back in time, even in memory
is to alter the altar of fangs where
meat offerings hung & dripped
songs to the longing earth.
A million flag songs might
be sung, but why if the old
ways are so gratefully dead?

IN THE COLONY

Blood sun drips
red licorice strips that
lash the longing earth
& I whisper the prayers
of a contented consumer.
I like the sun's warmth,
but I drool about those red
whips that accentuate our
slow darkness even though
it's rapidly becoming a white
light to me. I am a red ant
& swear I come from a red
ant world as I scurry & scatter
to nests made by things that
were never ants to begin with.

TEQUILA SUNRISE

In the tentacles of dream, clarity corn-
holed & dropped him outside the pre-
cincts of inky dawn. He'd returned to the
comic book of his heart to salvage simple
& sweet words when a poison-fanged
& polysyllabic *luchador* of reason caught
him in a naked chokehold. He scanned
the fading darkness one more time for *La
Llorona*, but she'd been deleted from the
scene so he stumbled out into the blaring
sun, a gleaming man of steel soon to rust.
He was not afraid.
Okay, he was.

WHEELS

The Paleolithic heart is obsidian, napped
to the sheen of the sun by men of metal.
There is no need to fall upon the sword
of belief. Our ancestors tell us we *were*
men of metal. We found native copper &
pounded it into little wheels. We made
roller skates & rolled into battle with other
tribes. We skated into buffalo hunts. We
circled the campfires on skates & as the
drums drummed on, we disco-danced the
nights away.

SAVAGE SUNSETS

Inside our darkening house
a spark of absurd realization:
I have not shaved this week.
I sigh deeply against the vague
& acrid accumulation of years.
A slow squeeze of sour house
air deadens moist memory.
I sit alone, waiting for night
to trump the blood of sunset.
I want to scurry from the bane
of this slow & shaded dance,
but I can't, Colleen, even
though I hear your voice
telling me to get my shit
together like you did before
the Alzheimer's swallowed
your tongue & touch. I smoke
& smoke & smoke in darkness
but the minor voodoo of cigarette
coals cannot put me in accord
with the sun undone.

NEBRASKA SCARLET FEVER

*In Boston, animals at the Franklin
Park Zoo were kept cool with sprin-
klers and frozen treats. The African
wild dogs and lions got frozen blood;
the primates received frozen fruit juice.*
                                 —CNN ONLINE

As insolent as Elvis,
the King of Beasts was
on his back, scruffy
scrotum at ease, gently
sucking a bloodsicle
& glaring at red-butt
baboons performing
perverse but cool tricks
with their fruitsicles.
Summer. East coast...

Dire heat reigned
in Nebraska too.
You were sleeping,
a light whistling
from your nose,
sweat on the brow.
I flicked off the tiny
television & fiddled
with the old AC with
little success so I trotted
to the Nurses' Station
but nobody was there

so I beat feet all the way
to the parking lot bathed
in my searing sadness &
the sunset's scarlet fever.
Driving home in the chill
of the almost exquisite
winter inside our bronze
Buick, teardrops froze,
fell to my lap & tinted
my testicles blue.

ESTÉBAN

Today I find my broken love nodded off
again in July heat with Estéban, that lame
ass, Zorro-looking fucktard on the *Home
Shopping Network* pimping his cheesy
guitars. My workman fingers were
always too fat to fit frets. I would never
be a Segovia. A drum might be my one &
only instrument, each lonely thump from
its drowsy heart, a segue into the nearest
cave with glyphs on the walls & love as
young & fresh as when first I found her.

DEGREES OF DROUGHT

Swirl of red air.
Swirl of red sun.
Into the oven we
dust beings dance &
pray someone feeds our
footprints a sidelong glance.

We know what
we know when
we know it.
That is what we say.
When we come
to know what
we did not know,
it is too late, so we
slur somber songs &
bring roses to ourselves.

Swirl of red rose.
We have coughed you up.

Swirl of red moon.
We have moaned at you.

We have measured all
degrees of drought.
Swirl of whirlwind.
Swirl of red blood.
Swirl of red memory.

Swirl of red woman.
Swirl of rattling
leaves raking sky.
Swirl of ravenous
roots raking earth.

Swirl of savage sunsets.
Swirl of the dead.
Somehow, still living.

———

Why sift the dust
looking for ghosts
when those ghosts
sift the same dust
looking for us?
They have mapped us,
measured & treasured us
while we huddled in the ether
of their mocking laughter.

BLACK LEATHER

The dignity of your daily
dying dazzles me, darling.
On the day of the final eclipse,
your angle of ascent from these
dire sand hills to *Canku Wakan*
will not be straight up, but
like an untied balloon freed &
zipping red in four directions.
There will be smiles because we
trained our minor insanities to
disdain the illusion of the linear
& accept that our eyes can betray.
Right now, if seen by Google's
spycam in space, I might seem
to be in quaint prayer, down
on my knees in the dark &
dusty closet of a room I can
no longer sleep in, but flashlight
in hand, I am searching, sorting
through your shoes, looking for
a good candidate to cut a corner
out of & give your hammer toe
some relief when I stumble
onto your black leather boots.
Unused in a dozen years,
the leather is supple & shockingly
soft like a ghost kick to the nuts.

SUN/DANCE/SONG

I met my first love at thirteen.
She was brown & I was pretty green.
—Eric Burdon

Born dead this spring,
an ancient & skeletal elm
in our backyard scratches
the face of the sullen sun.
Sliced ribbons of sunlight
wrap the fact that nothing
can save you this dry July,
not even bleeding dancers
tethered by medicine prayers
to a freshly cut cottonwood
tree twenty miles from here.

Faces skyward, we all seek
songs in the whirlwinds
that parch our slow lives.
We pray all songs for divine
reversal of flesh destructed
will be honored by the sun,
auburn, ancient & savage.

RED-HEADED DEVILS

A fat, sweating aide
with flaming red hair
& greasy, old sneakers
chases me out of your
cell so she can change
your diaper so I go out
to the patio to smoke &
fret & fume for a while.
I stand above an anemic
rose bush & one flower
has a bee sacked out in
a bright, crimson vortex.
Maybe the thing is dead.
I drop ashes on its head
trying to get movement
& nothing breathes but
the shadows behind me.

A geezer with dyed red
hair & a thinned out DA
bums a smoke so I light
the coffin nail & wedge
it in his palsied fingers
& he hotboxes it like he
had three pairs of lungs.
His huge amber eyes are
so grateful that when he
asks for another I fulfill
his desire but then I

get chewed out by yet
another huge aide with
fiery red hair & bad skin
for an illegal ignition in Hell.

He only gets one an hour.

Which of us knows what
words will ring in eternity?

He only gets one an hour.

I peer down at the rose that
cages the bee, cages me in
stagnant Nebraska breath
while the two obese aides
convene in whisper & scowl.
This axis of evil, these two
red-headed devils chattering
is not a good sign, but they
allow me back in your room
where your silent & circular
smile catches me halfway
between shudder & sigh.

BLUE FOG

The night is brittle & hot
when a crazed fly lands
on your face so I roll
up a magazine & swipe
at it & nick your nose &
you don't fucking move.
Brittle & hot, this night
& your feet are so cold
& blue mere minutes
after your baby steps
upon the Ghost Road.

Four hours later I am
home, sitting in the dark.
Softly discordant & almost
anomalous on these Plains,
a blue fog creeps in & climbs
onto your tan cashmere sweater
there in the closet, the one
I've guarded from moths
these past twelve years.

Blue fog or tinted cashmere.
What shall we bury you in
besides the flimsy shroud
of these pale words?

CLOUDLESSNESS

This cloudless day
I am not tethered by
any traces of Tanqueray.
My clear eyes catch millions
of invisible devils dancing
in a bestial blue sky—it's
beyond irony how clear
eyes can perfect the grace
of callous cloudlessness.

Cloudlessness is such
a big, fat hollow word,
but it contains the power
to make green memory
brittle–it can force yellow
prairies to beg for a final
fuck by furious wildfire.

Death of a loved one does
not mean the death of love,
I said with clichéd hands
tainted with juniper flames
& raised to the aimless blue
serenity of a Christian sky.
My sweating essence, that
very need for prayer came

via an aversion to Jehovah
but the God dog in His
insufferable indolence
& need to represent,
pretended to understand,
to be (like His great red,
white & blue host)
all that He could be
so, I whimpered,
& yes, acquiesced.

In month nine of the sixth
year of this feeble century,
smoke rose from my flesh
to impregnate a fallow sky
but not one cloud formed.
My blood moaned thick
with words but the sky
was fickle, eternally bored
with decades of dry-humping
the limp Republic of Metaphor.

Cante Wasté Win.

In your churning
Lakota sky an absence
of big, chubby clouds
made the miserable day
all the more miserable.

There were *no* cartoon
clouds demanding that
I look heavenward for
your soft, loving face.
I didn't have to—you
were up there, serene
& free of pain & your
cool shade protected
me when they handed
me the shovel & I began
ladling the dry Wakpamni
soil onto your rough box
until it was time to hand
the tool to your many
blood-dark relations
whose lives will continue
to flow & feed our ancient
& flesh-hungry Indian earth.

EL DÍA DE LOS MUERTOS

Due to some sappy miscalculation of the *ofrenda,* a skull arose between my shoulders tonight like a white balloon with a short string tether so I named the little devil Señor Skull.

Señor Skull is ghoulish & garish & slightly gay in an awkward way as he bloodies his aching mouth with my dead wife's lipstick. I don't know if it's sad or amusing, his fat lips pursed into a crimson kiss, its dying warmth rising, so carelessly cultivating the black, starless sky.

THE TATTERED FLAGS
OF THE FOUR DIRECTIONS

1. *YELLOW*

Dancing yellow, larger
than my hand, a butterfly
the color of butter slaps
against my face as I step
out the front door on
the way to your wake.
Startled by the bright
attack, I swat the insect
& it falls to the ground.
I rub it with my foot
until there is no trace
of vibrant fluttering
& unexpected beauty.
The world goes dark.

2. *BLACK*

That night…
of your ultimate oversleep
the cheesy Catholic priest,
imperious yet wearing shorts,
said, "She will not suffer her
daily pain" & gave prayers
of repose, commending your
spirit to God & was almost

done with his babble when
his portable oxygen unit
started making incredibly
loud fart noises & I swear
I thought you might rise
from the dead in a fit
of wild, rez-girl laughter.
The image of your smile
held me for a minute &
then black, raging waters
swept me down stream.

3. *RED*

In this drawer, a calendar
from Rapid City Chevrolet
has a photo glued on of
you standing with your
new Chevy Celebrity,
five full years before
Alzheimer's disheveled us.
Beaming girl, brilliant smile.
Daughter of a rez bootlegger,
former nun & present teacher,
you wanted one in flaming red.
I said charcoal suited you better
& any new car is intoxicating to
a child of poverty so you did
smile wildly in the photo, but
later would only refer to your
purchase as "the gray car."

So add "the gray car" to my
list of mistakes & regrets.
I should have known better,
should have known the treaties
entitled all Sioux to horses of flame.

4. WHITE

In "the gray car"
driving north on BIA 27
through dried palomino
hills & admiring the smoky
burgundy of sunset reflecting
off my taut biceps, I come
upon a wounded jackrabbit
doing a spasm dance in
the middle of the road.
I stop & help it hop to
the shoulder where I say
kind words to its broken head
& wait for it to give up the ghost.
Nightfall comes & still it dances.
Dance of madness, dance of pain,
a dance of gain & two steps back.
It dervishes for twelve, long years
until it finally wearies of spinning.
Diminished, I get back in my car.
Moonlight sifts my hair, now white,
& darkness hides my trembling hands.

LOVE THE DISTANT ROAR

Love all the train wrecks
in savage rearview mirrors.
Love any hush of sadness,
any dark breath made from
the bullying glee of accomplices
who have sold their half-hearted
kisses for treaties, for crystal meth,
for love & resurrection, whatever,
whatever it takes to survive.
Love the contrivance of bells
heralding any small healing.
Love the distant roar
of the skin you're in.
Love the distant roar
of the sin you've been.

COWBOYS &

Outside my pastures
of gray, the sacred cow
of war is being milked
dry by those hairless
cowboys of my generation
who never got laid or high.
Done milking, they cloak
the old bovine with banners,
bang & splay her, spread her
legs & birth a hundred thousand
devil dogs marching to the udder
beat of a little black book, deployed
simply to suck out the marrow
of the ancient bone-tribes.
I cannot pretend otherwise,
cannot pretend it's not how
the white man rolls.

BROTHER BEAR

Brother Bear,
tonight the pale &
quivering moon of bone
illuminates our return to
the sweetest human form,
whole in our land of ancestors,
whole among the green sage
& the peacefully starving
jackrabbits of memory.
Heart attack? Maybe.
Some discordant spirit
whispers, "Passed out &
froze in the cab of his truck."
It is an impossible concept.
You are *only* ten years old,
standing here in the dusk
trying to catch the passes,
the punts that I practice.

for Jerry

SEÑOR SKULL'S PARADE

An arid spheroid, devoid
of flesh & soul arises again
& grins upon my shoulders.
He is the *luchador* of bone.
I am a *luchador* of flesh &
by virtue of an iPod we
march to zydeco washboards
& accordions round & round
our quaint kitchen table.

Our skull parade has started.
It's luscious & scary & if I were
still young I wouldn't quite
comprehend the deliciousness
of mounting piles of things in
the house: bundled newspapers,
old clothes, even new clothes with
labels attached, the unread books
of lonely poets, washed & saved
margarine containers, drawers
of plastic sporks & hundreds
of Wendy's ketchup packets.
So this is how I will die...
My spirit will lurch down
canyons of unread magazines,
a hot, dry wind at my back &
a shrieking chorus of feral cats,
so pissed & clump-haired that

it will take a swat team of SPCA
wranglers to round them up
upon my silent demise.
I turn off the iPod.

＊＊＊

Today at work a white girl,
a secretary I like too much
said (half in jest, I hope),
"Do a rain dance. It's been
so dry & my tomatoes—"
Yes, do a "rain dance."
As if . . . As (fucking) if . . .
my blood contained all
azimuths of red arcana
& I could produce such
utilitarian wetness at will.
"I wish I could," I said, but
jack-in-the-box Señor Skull
snorted out a snide aside:
Darling, tonight I'm going to
sneak into your pale garden
& cornhole your tomatoes,
make them wet & juicy
one moaning globe at a time.

Of course, I couldn't say *that*.

I'm a mellower wine now.
Age has rendered me sweet
& dry & drought suits all
skeletal beings, but don't get

me totally wrong—I can still
rain on any dickwad's parade
even if I am that dickwad.
Rain clouds *are* in my blood.
My blood is in rain clouds.

———⋙⋘———

When I was six some deliriously
liquored up local Skins ran over
the legs of two white cowboys
after they'd stabbed them dead.
When I asked a cousin why,
he shrugged, winked & said,
"Because ghosts can't chase
you with broke-ass legs."
As if . . . my heart should have
known such blood-fool magic.
As if . . . anyone's heart knew
every riddle between the dryness
of here & the looming hereafter.
As if . . . I would never march
daftly in Señor Skull's parade.

RESPITE

Breathe deeply. Inhale.
Chew slowly the pill of respite.
You are becoming sleepy.
You are becoming sleepy.
Your eyelids are very heavy.
Imagine water, peaceful water.
Water slicing through green land.
A water knife, pure & sanctified.
Breathe deeply. Inhale.

Chiloquin, Oregon 1954.
The story could be set here
or anywhere actually, let's
just say there *is* a place.

There *is* a place or
maybe there *was* a place.
That's more accurate.
Everything beautiful
eventually turns cannibal.
Beauty is as beautiful does.
Stream. Stream, clear as sky.
Stream. Water bucket clean.
Stream. Blue with giant rainbow
swimming as if in cloudless air.
Stream. A brass hook baited
with a clump of white bread.
Rainbow. Lunkers lurk with
fisheyes of greatest contempt,

aware of their own irrelevancy
& aware of the boy's magazine.
Boy. Sitting on a clover patch,
half dozing under sleepier sun.
Beaver. Hairy, funky, pissed.
Beaver. On the hook, furious
yellow teeth bared & ready to
take names, jumps on the bank.
Boy. On the run, willow pole lost.
On the run, dirty magazine lost too.
Boy. Safe in a pine forest, sits
& lights a pilfered Pall Mall.
He breathes deeply. Inhales
the mist of metacognition.

AT SIOUX MONUMENT

At Sioux Monument one mile
past Martin on SD Highway 73
recent tribal history is indexed
in the long row of tombstones.
Granite from as far away as
Pennsylvania protrudes from
old snow in this, the saddest
of all Lakota winter counts.
But, there are no loved ones
asleep under these markers.
Here lie unpaid balances, due
upon delivery of stone to grave.
Here lie the hearts of families
fractured by cosmic poverty.

BLACK OUT

Black out.
My headlights scare up
two skinny cedars, loitering
nervously upon the tired snow.
On these plains, historical winds
have raped all trees & minds.
Swirling flakes backlit make
me cry like a motherless child.
We all eat clichés in this universe.
If we lie to people we do not even
know, then we'll lie to ourselves.
Half of mourning, the darkest part
is that fearing for our own deaths.
Before me lies a mound of dirt &
I could layer lie upon lie & say
that in this instant I smell beans
& ham hocks, hear her laughter
above clinking wine glasses & rez
dogs courting a quaint red moon,
but I don't. It's too black out.

SUNSET AT THE INDIAN CEMETERY

Not one of these red seeds
planted will ever sprout.
Pray for them.

A chunk of yellow fat,
the winter sun is circled
by gaunt prairie crows.
Pray for the crows.

Pray into the lung-
shocking wind shrieking
so fucking freakishly into
these boundless yucca hills.

Pray for all those who believe
our DNA is forever tainted
by the comic, brilliant truth
that we have been here
forever, maybe longer.

MOURNING LOG

Back in Monsantoville, MN,
summer stops slipping it
to fall & pale winter is born.
New snow slows all chaos
so I dump last night's chili
(not the best batch ever)
in the driveway for crows.
Soon they'll explode darkly
upon this white, little town.
I'm simply a faceless idiot
in a nation of faceless idiots.
I drink powdered espresso &
watch an obese neighbor lady
mutter past my house, her
porky English bulldog sports
orange knit booties & when I
smile, the spirit scab thickens
atop this zombie chest where
my heart once loyally lingered.

HORSE ACADEMY

Oh my, but you have a pretty face.
You favor a girl that I knew.
— JESSE WINCHESTER

We smoke & shiver together.
She's all big-boned & horsey,
a glorious gelding of a gal
whose name I don't know.
We chatter on the unsalted
sidewalk outside my office.
She has a bandaged finger
& says she was attacked by
a violent cactus she got free
from the botany greenhouse.
"They were going to toss it–a
little prick can make you numb."

A little prick can make you numb.
She is eighteen & the only thing
that registers on her gray matter
is the kindly gray haze standing
beside her & said haze, realizing
the true nature of his penance,
stubs out his smoke & canters
back inside to the warmth
of his gray, unearthly stall
& dozes off behind his desk.

THE LATE NIGHT MOVIE IN
MY SMALL AMERICAN BRAIN

Soon a squamus sun will
knock softly on my door.
Then I will deftly pull
the dreary drapes or put
on shades for the show.
But for now it's a couch,
microwave popcorn &
metaphorical meanderings
in the Carpathians where
antiquarian menfolk are
settled in for the night,
slant-drilling far beyond
their plump *hausfraus* &
into the phantasmagorical.
Up the road, in the castle,
the throbbing woofers of
vampirical testosterone
provide the bass for any
tune of testy imperative.

MY BOSSES ARE HEIFERS

These bitches deny me bereavement leave.

Drab of spirit, blowzy, these
women are my bosses, they
of the milk maid variety,
they of the gingham panties,
hand-hewn & huge, frowzy
& drubbed, scrubbed white
as light for their frightful God
& I must do as they say.

In bovine body & soul
my bosses are heifers, blind to
their ancestors ghost-tethered
to Conestogas, dull bells
dangling from their necks.
My bosses cannot fathom
such a moping & mooing
history upon these dusty Plains
where peace-loving redskins
grumbled mildly & waited for
the parade to pass, anxious to
get back to their cribbage &
martinis, shaken, not stirred.

A FRAGILE CHANT OF HOLY AIR

Waiting for blood pressure
pills, I sneak a smoke outside
the clinic & am startled by a
sky blue whirlybird making
dust as it rises into cotton
candy clouds which fail
to make my heart drool.
Somebody's loved one is
up there, a body in a sky
blue chopper rising from
the IHS hospital heliport.
Some body is broken.
Some body is screwed,
blued & tattooed like
a lost prayer to Heaven.
Hey. Hey! *Hey a hey…*

I fire up another smoke &
watch a blue machine pierce
clouds turned pink as blond
catkins by sunset's stealth.
It's beginning to snow &
I don't know if I'm crying
or not because I can't see
out the windows of this
helicopter that is my head.
Fat head, man head, dead
head with ghost hair dancing
down to my ample waist.

On another planet ten yards
away, a flock of folks I do not
know are smoking & crying
outside the emergency room.

Lord, we are all so lost in
our fragile chants of holy air.
Please help us... if you have
the power, the *huevos*, whatever
you call the coin of your realm.

AVOIDING HARMONIC CONVERGENCE
IN SIOUX FALLS, SOUTH DAKOTA

Life in the graying world...
What sleep you had was black
& dreamless, paralytic without
any conjured lover's cum-drip-lips.
So, why (on this first week of summer
release, in this tenth year of Minnesota imprisonment)
did a jesting anachronism
of morning wood wake you up & down?
Scavenging blue jays peck rheumy eyes
fully open & already bored with the corn
town morning, you get into line behind
Stepford wives in mini-vans & drive to
Starbuck's where the coffee's the same
as it was yesterday & the day before.
You may not even be there. Really.
You might be an old ghost catching
itself doing youthful tricks in a mirror,
a prisoner to its patterns, locked into
familiar paths where it haunts itself.

Daily pills washed down, you decide
to cruise to Sioux Falls & the sweetness
of a young healer's soft, brown hands.
Old fool, old fart, flashing down tar laid
through mutant cornfields though your
left front tire is low, no shimmy but that
distinct vibration emanating from tread

on up to your decrepit butt only kneads
your brain with visions of dark hands
Dark girl said never write her down.

So really, you don't want a poem &
she wants no poem so there is not a
march of pissant words toward anything
remotely logical, visionary, or beautiful.
You are not looking for such a simplistic
hand job though you have nothing against
a good KY performance & yes, you know
everyone has his own definition of truth.
Yours is this: you are simply hurtling
your ancient Ford Crown Victoria
towards her & her city (not your city).
You are listening to a Tim Buckley tune
from the shadows of your most wayward
youth that you bought three decades later
via iTunes. Why did you purchase it?
What memory blood were you looking
to siphon? What carcass to fang & defile?

Sometimes I wonder...
just for a while...
will you remember me?

Then you hear an almost requisite scoring
of blades, choppers from the SD Air Guard
overhead the very second you pull off I-90
at the SF airport exit. At the base of a down
ramp, a funky dude in crusty Levi's squats
upon a battered duffel bag & for an instant
you are deathly afraid you know him.

The bearded man holds a cardboard
sign in his grimy hands:

```
FREE POEMS
BY JACK DANIEL
VIETNAM VET
6/15 FA
NEEDS WORK
PLEASE HELP
```

Jack Daniel? The comic moniker icing
on an almost panic-inducing overload,
the Buckley war years anthem with
loud choppers overhead, the sad
& loony vet peering into your skull.
What type of bored dickhead would sit
down & devise such pathetic contrivance?

Okay, maybe you might, but it is
a semi-harmonic convergence too
good to be true & too true to be good.
Unreal, actually. You could have sat for
hours molding, fabricating such a clichéd
scenario & verily the vet's name might
be a clue to the fact of such hallucination.
Jack Daniel. Too redolent of blur & too
close to your whiskey facts, *but* the dude
holds a thick sheaf of poems in one hand.
You can feel Jack's harsh stare stab into
your stomach & out your rear as you
hit the stoplight. *A ghost on patrol?*
A befuddled spirit? You stare straight

ahead, straight ahead with blinders on.
You have to, you're on your way to her
& her healing medicine of sadness salve
& you are not going to crawl across
some Vietnam vet's crazed rice paddy.
You have your own brain worms
to deal with, but had you the means
you would make a sign, yes, a mirrored
glyph of madness to flash back at Jack:

```
I'M IN A HURRY
TO TOUCH
SOMETHING FURRY.
CATCH YOU
ON THE REBOUND
IF YOU ARE
STILL AROUND.
```

You don't want a poem now & often never
& damn it this is no poem. Whatever *his*
poems said, the words were his, not yours
& you are driving purposefully with a low
tire in a new century in which poets & their
products are more often than not useless &
embarrassing antiques. But you wish you'd
bought a poem from the broke poet-vet.
You wish him good sales & all the luck he
deserves in this kingdom of brief regrets
& constant wars. Sad-ass fools, you both.

So, *this* is your report after returning home
after waiting two hours on her front porch
after getting no touch after driving back up

that same on ramp & seeing no Jack Daniel
there, but goddamn it, you wish you could
tell the man that you were led astray by
the magneto of moon pie & you hope
he will forgive your hunger
& you will look for him on
your next patrol... you promise,
yes, yes, you do, but you
know that you won't.

OPPRESSION INVOCATION

Sirs, please
find my drab ass
in that final hour.
Shine it like Aztec
gold under whitecaps
off the Dry Tortugas.
Adhere me to the cross
of alchemical resurrection
& I will snake dance to tin
pipes playing Garryowen
without any cloaking device
constructed of eagle feathers.
My smile will be immaculate.
The asp I grasp will be turgid
& glistening with Biblical tears.
I swear. I swear I'll be
all that is holy.

FLAG SONG

I shouldn't speak of the dead,
but yes, I knew them well.
They had a small flagpole,
old glory upside down
above their tattered yard.
Yeah, they lived between
the hammer of liquor &
the anvil of poverty & they
had little choice but to name
their shrieking flesh *love*.
Annealed, they thought
they could heal any frailty
carried within them, but
they could not & wasted
valuable arrows pricking
the dead flesh of God.
Yes, I knew them well.
They had a small flagpole
that pierced the flaccid
flank of our ancient earth.

ANOTHER DAY IN THE KINGDOM

Of course my invisibility guaranteed
invisibility to anything I wore or held,
once I chose to turn the power on.
I loved the heft of the needle-nosed
pliers, unseen as me when I wafted
through the crowd, gently breezing
the asses of beautiful women until I
climbed the dais & pinched the King's
balls with those pliers & as he howled
I did the same to his mechanical wife.
Of course the secret agents ran amok
in a gigantic, sun-glassed clusterfuck,
but the King remained the King
& when I became visible I
remained invisible.

PROFESSIONAL DEVELOPMENT PLAN

Dire days, these. My eyes avert the pert pouts of pretty derrières. Nothing tastes as it should. Prime rib becomes bologna & good merlot grape Kool-aid. Some days I find myself lurking upon a gravel road, waiting for a dark car of proper vintage to tamp my old soul down & if things go according to plan the wild young man driving the car into me will be me. Delicious & queerly exciting.

I THOUGHT I SAW DICK CHENEY
CHASING A BUS IN MINNEAPOLIS

I thought I saw Dick Cheney
chasing a bus in Minneapolis.
He looked just like himself &
was wearing baggy new Levi's
with one of those chain things
hooked to a belt loop & then to
his wallet & God I'd never wear
such a gizmo as this old bastard
who was huffing & puffing through
traffic unaware his head was nearly bald
& his ponytail was constructed of neck hair.
I wanted to sneak up & ask if he were fatally
worn out from fucking his beloved country,
ask if he had enjoyed playing the player, but
he jumped on the bus & was gone, gone, gone.

NATIVITY

Baby Jesus,
I do so love
this prairie wind, how it
unsheathes obsidian knives
cloaked in starlight & allows
whispered threats of castration to shiver
the dull spires of your little white churches.

TOLLEFSON'S RAKE

I shattered my bamboo
lawn rake on late spring snow
& was too lazy this summer to
haul my ass to Hardware Hank.
I don't need a rake in summer.
A student crew does my lawn,
but so far this year I have hired
no one to rake the leaves & it's
October already & I'm outside
kicking at a pile of maple leaves
herded upon my sidewalk when
Tollefson, my neighbor, exits his
back door & strolls into my yard.

Clad in an ancient fatigue jacket,
he offers to let me use his rake.
"No, man, it's okay," I say.
"Dude, you need it," he says.
I bore into his pixilated blue eyes
& say, "No. Thank you, but no."
He keeps standing there. So do
I, waiting for the impasse to end.
He says the Hmong college girls
next door partied loud last night.
He calls them "Mungolians" & I
fight hard to keep from smiling.
"Sideways stuff takes me back,"
he says & I wince & try to recall
when my brain was iron, how it

felt to smash through the soft
human world with a hard
American head, but I can't
so I simply nod & resume kicking
at the mound of blood-red leaves &
ignore Tollefson, who trembles in
damp silence in a shitty rice paddy
thirty miles south of Da Nang
with friends bleeding out.

I tap him on his shoulder.
"Okay, I'll use your rake," I say.

MANTLE

If Einstein & Frankenstein had backdoor
sex, their lovechild would be the gleaming
black Dodge Ram Mega Cab® pickup in
front of me. Showroom-new with chrome
up the wazoo, it's the ultimate bling-beast
of burden. But all that I want from capital-
ism is a new Mr. Coffee® to take the morn-
ing cobwebs away & I'm on my way to buy
one. The kid piloting the beastly Dodge in
the Wal-Mart parking lot wears a Yankees
cap askew, hip-hop style & dangling from
the trailer hitch below the back bumper is a
huge set of chrome testicles. I'm somewhat
nut-thrashed into awe & torpor, so I let him
take the parking space I'd been coveting.
Ok, Lord, let him believe in the ephemeral
magic of the shining scrotum. A quaint &
ancient autumn is painting the ash trees &
the ghost of Mickey Mantle is swinging in
my brain.

THE RESURRECTION OF ELVIS

Mediocrity surrounds itself
with, well, you guessed it.
That's always the case, like
goobers that smirked about
my heavy sweat in a brutish,
butt-breathing way & said:
*Oh, he weren't the same after
such & such...* Damn, I wasn't
the same before & in fact was
never the same *ever* & when
their children take communion
in stinky toe, tree-top Tennessee,
I'll rip a vein from my Johnson,
jam it in their eyes & they'll see
me, miraculous in the dogwoods,
wearing a sparkly crown of stars.

ARCANE AIRS ON PHILLIPS AVE.

To shimmy & blear in the specter of crank.
To be fat & skanky, wearing black tights
& a pink halter top in the August night.
To be poor, to be poor forever & to have
a homemade, prison tattoo barely visible
upon brown & once-venerable skin.
To be a full-throated dick warbler
among the red-necked peckers
of Sioux Falls & to wobble so
purposefully upon paved
plains, a warrior in
white high heels.

THE WARPATH

Time is the school in which we learn
Time is the fire in which we burn.
        —DELMORE SCHWARTZ

The devil's pitchfork
of dry lightning impregnates
arid hills & flame piranhas
swim manically up & down
Ponderosa canyons & across
prairie grassland until a black
sky ruptures upon a black land.
Several peaceful days pass &
prayers against calamity cease.

Fire...
living dormant in the earth,
actually residing in the soil
a few days after prairie rains
somehow reincarnates itself,
crawls up a tree & intoxicated
with the view blazes the crowns
of a thousand other ancient pines.

Fire...
re-birthed, explodes into radio
& a local AM station captures
one old rancher on a call-in
line, saying he will never
abandon his flaming ranch.
"My family's been here
for four generations."

Four generations.

It's all too fucking perfect when
a small town radio newsman
segues into a live patch with
firefighters who are part of
an Indian "Hotshot" crew.

In smoke-soaked yellow
shirts they circle the white
man's land, flutter their weary
eyelids, notch their arrows &
wait to reclaim what they never
claimed to own in the first place.
The signal to attack is given.
The war chief lights a cigar,
holds up four fingers & says
something that makes his warriors
roar with gut-wrenching laughter,
something about his ex-wife & two
monkeys in a Denver bar room.

MOONLIGHT RANCH: 1965

Beer-pillaged,
we sped down
the gravel roads
into the shadows,
turned off the ignition
& exited into a cavern.
Faint burgundy pictures
tacked to the velvet walls
of our brains were drawn in
long-dried blood, but real live
flesh stunned us, stole our voices.
We giggled & our damp hands could
not stop shaking when the shadows
from corner pews sang their humid
breath of song so sweet we had to
gorge our thumbs into our ears.
Dirge or anthem, we learned
to dance, the holy squirting
dance of life.

APPROXIMATE HAIKU, 1976

Pathetic how now comes
memory like little bubblings
circling the head of some
drunken cartoon character...
Except I *knew* my bubbles
were angels, not soaplings.
Then, foolishly, I still believed
in the power of ghost shirts.
Back then I was invincible.
When the fat checkout girl
said my two T-Bones were
"yummy-looking," I said I
would cook dinner for her.
Then she saw my buzzing
angels & shuddered when
I said, "You can chew the
steaks & I'll chew on you."
She called the manager
who told me to leave.
My *no* to him meant *yes*
to approximate haiku:
two cold Big Macs in
the Sioux Falls slammer.

JUNE 1876, MONTANA

Artemisia tridentata, "tall sage"
blooms Vesper Sparrows
on a warm June morning.
Varied trilling reams the air.
Ass Hole is there. So is Rectum
& a host of angry red pricks.
Yes, Ear Ring Prick is there.
So is Little Prick & Neck Prick.
Sing Prick is there & who
could forget Soft Prick?
Ha! Snatch Loser is there.
Vesper Sparrows scream
in a blue sky & the sun
is a brand new penny.
It is a good day—

THE WART OF SATAN

"Never bring the Lord an animal that is blind, has broken bones, cuts, warts, scabs, or ringworm. Never give the Lord any of these in a sacrifice by fire on the altar."

—*LEVITICUS 22:22*

I offered my broken spirit to the Lord & he ignored me so I waddled inexorably towards the black light.

———

Somewhere between Immaculate Conception & wireless reception, the Wart of Satan was born. Oh, fearsome wart, I am old & tired. Don't talk down & dirty to me.

———

Blessed be your "snow day" inception when I was alone at home with the tube & the lube & finished, trumped the desperation of the Last Supper with homemade beef stew aged in the freezer for two wart-less years.

———

The boxer interviewed said, "I want to inflect damage once I step into the ring." *The Wart of Satan comprehends all snot-knocking epiphanies.*

In Ecclesiastes it says, "When a wart becomes bed bound upon your nose, do not despair. It has only chosen you as its Lord."

In Murderapolis, I hear the Pillsbury doughboy on Public Radio moan the blues so far off-key that winos puking blood would be a sweeter music. *Wart of Satan, go thee to him.*

Were I to conjure a winter count, it would speak of a green, green valley where two bears danced down a road covered with dusty toads, each step an explosion of toad ghosts & warts.

Blessed be the dawn & its expurgation of historical facts. But how should I react to the minor cruelty of a devil's ship, a Mayflower landing upon my nose?

The store bought remedy lacks poetics & is quite unlike a needed scalping. It's more like peeling back the skullcap & peeing on one's brain. *This is your brain on drugs.*

I am no snitch (simply something of a witch with a cursed proboscis) but I hereby confess that I am attempting to murder the Wart of Satan.

It has happened. Poof. Gone. Wart...merely a whisper in my silver sky of age. My flesh fluttered, rose, tasted rain & stalled in a morose lack of antagonism. It came with the dust... & was gone with the wind.

This sense of bereavement is awkwardly odd. Caught in a graceless angle of vanity, I was weak when I wanted it gone. Wart, you most surely were flesh of my flesh & I mourn you & our little war.

HORSEHIDE

At my martini limit,
I come face to face
with a typically lame
Freshman essay holding
a plenitude of platitudes
in drippy, run-on sentences
that feature tense changes
& ampersands plus a lexicon
of abused or misspelled words.

The kid, mostly silent in class,
is rambling about his lifelong
love of baseball & it must be
the ghost of horsehide on
my fingertips that glides,
warps the breaking curve
of a C into an A & then I
slide into bed, safe at home.

ARCADIA

I.

To rejoin the circle,
you ran from rust cities
into rusticity, knowing
iron, even in the last throes
of youth, would not bend.
Gleaming, you stood before
bedroom mirrors & prayed
to the spirit of shine, knowing
the air you breathed could betray.

II.

You & the ghost of your wife
found an ancient knife on
a forgotten western battlefield.
Maybe the old iron had cried &
contaminated itself—maybe it did not.
Maybe, it taught the blue skies to lie,
to whisper that lust was powdered
blood & needed tears to grow.

THE ARC OF IT ALL

A flock of geese
forms a circle &
rolls into sunset.

Sweat, blood & fears.
Steel fused to hand
chills the bones until

a sliver of moon
rises & melts with
morning coffee.

You make the bed
& tuck a Ruger .327
under the extra pillow.

The brain snuggling
in your skullcap believes
that ghosts sleep deeply

in daylight.

ARC OF THE COVEN

When the scent of death
tainted a desert dream,
they swooped down, faces
red & eerie, black feathers
hiding their blacker hearts
& pecked & pecked against
an unmoving copper corpse.
"Oh love," they screeched.
"Oh blood," they blathered.
Copper, lacking any irony,
offered a simple tolling,
a laughing echo of beaks
thrust in mindless hunger.

It knocked the wind
from my nuts when
those cloaked in love
& trust became vultures.

GHOST ROAD

Somewhere
nowhere &
her not here
& nothing but
a weird & weary
recitation of ever
changing songs
to a whole brain
to a broken brain
to a dead brain
to a ghost brain.
In dreams I wait
for the ghost brain
to devour the broken
& become whole again.
I am no factotum of despair.
I do worship ancient hungers
& chins dribbling blood, but I'm
damn tired of the taste of my heart.

DARK LIGHT

Miniaturized, the sun
is a blood egg, a blip
on the flat horizon.
My shadow is ancient
and drags ancient balls
through pungent & pale
sage rooted in bad dirt.
Years ago I swear I
could write my initials
with a urine stream, but
now bad dirt, its alkaline
crust dusted with weak
spring snow erases me,
erases my walking prayer
to the dark light of home.

INDIAN COWGIRL IN SPACE

Itchy songs in the soil
gave her fifty-five years
of stomping, mad dancing
barefoot upon the alien planet.
Until. Finally. Black-fanged
bloodworms pierced her flesh
& she became alienated too.
Alien unto alien begets
sex fiend sex. Incest.
Insect lust. The stars first.
The stars & then the worms
& now such small applause for her
apoplectic & beautiful bucking end.

THUNDER SNOW

Thunder snow.
Wizard blizzard.
The white hair frost is
congregating at the temples
& I have not thawed a single
soul in three long years.

Okay, everybody sing.

Monja, Monja.
I want your big begonia.

*The phantom limb still
seeks acknowledgment
years after amputation.*

THE MENU

*SIOUX FALLS -- Death row inmate Elijah
Page chose steak and salad for his last meal,
which was served about 4:50 p.m. CST.
The menu consisted of steak with A1 Steak
Sauce, jalapeño poppers with cream sauce,
onion rings, salad with cherry tomatoes, ham
chunks, shredded cheese, bacon bits, ranch and
bleu cheese dressing, lemon iced tea, coffee and
ice cream. Page, who confessed to murdering
Chester Allan Poage near Spearfish is sched-
uled to die at 10 p.m. CDT tonight.*
      —RAPID CITY JOURNAL

Iced tea & ice cream.
Ham chunks & bacon bits.
We are a mundane people
living upon mundane plains.
We dine upon the mundane
& forget to pray for our
sad-ass, mundane selves.

Nevertheless, last year there
were 2.75 million cattle lurking
upon South Dakota dirt & they
give this poor slob a slab that
he has to slather with A-1.

It is not yet tomato season,
cherry or otherwise, but
cherry tomatoes & death?
A combo beyond poetry &
I'd bet my left nut that his
bleu cheese dressing came

from a plastic squeeze bottle.
Everything else seems duly
clogged with bad cholesterol,
but all in all, the menu makes
me very, very hungry for
the blood of the dead &
if it were my last meal
I suppose I would relish it.

Colleen, my love,
I do not recall what I ate
on the day of our death.

I would like to think that
what I ate the day you died
was cold, greasy & perfunctory,
but I really cannot remember.
I suppose our histories matter
only to us for a short while
& then they matter to no one.

Last week I got a honeydew
melon that was sour inside.
I threw the two halves into
the backyard for the birds.
Between peck & shrivel, all
hints of green soon vanished.
Thin, brown skins left with
a broom wind that brought
strong thunder & weak rain.
When it thundered last night,

it sounded exactly like huge,
human farts. Exactly...
A result of global warming?
I may be close to the edge.

Driving to Starbuck's today,
I passed an old duo in a Buick.
Woman was yapping at man
just like a Chihuahua would &
I know man was thinking of
A-1 on his steak reward for
tolerating the years of peck
& shrivel, the strong thunder
of her voice, the weak
rain of his aging groin.

----◾◾◾----

Menu: One year memorial.
Slim Buttes, SD. Brittle, brutal August.
I'm early & lay claim to a plastic
chair close to the grill & prairie wind
wind whips charcoal smoke directly
into my thrashing brain & the scene
turns slow & I don't know why
your family always chars burgers
black & within a half hour I'm so
stoned on briquettes & Pepsi that
my loving fear of ghosts dissipates.
When I leave at dusk, I move
slowly, dryly like a walking
piece of withered jerky.

THE END OF THE TRAIL IS
A BEGINNING OF THE TRAIL

I wasn't some troll caged by
the gravity of a dank bridge,
but I was compressed under
the arc of a whitening sky
when I heard them whisper.

"We like him somewhat.
He knows to fart precisely
the moment the saddle rises."

The dumb bastards did not
know I always rode bareback
& spoke their secret tongue.
I'd loitered in their mother's
womb, had suckled her books
in her oak-leathered rooms.

My haggard horse hung low
his head, his neck my pillow
& his back was my bed.
"Fine," they said. "Sleep
deep & bring us a dream."

So we did & we were running
in shimmering delight, delirious
in the strength of our youth.
Our fertile flanks foamed in
the sunlight & our hooves did
not skitter when we hit rocks.

Past the stones & onto sand,
we whirled, dashed around
& over rabbit brush & sage
& heard voices that seemed to
come from the whitening sky.
"You bring us a dream. You
& not that goddamned nag."

They did not know the horse
& I were one blood, one bone.
Such purchase was beyond
their deep pockets so we ran
& ran like a son of a bitch
until the sky reddened &
we stalled in a sentence
of sweat & self-love.

ABOUT THE AUTHOR

A half-breed Indian, Adrian C. Louis was born and raised in northern Nevada and is an enrolled member of the Lovelock Paiute Tribe. From 1984-97, Louis taught at Oglala Lakota College on the Pine Ridge Reservation of South Dakota. Earlier, he edited four Native newspapers including *The Lakota Times* and later *Indian Country Today.* Currently, Louis is Professor of English at Minnesota State University in Marshall. He has written twelve books of poems and two works of fiction: *Wild Indians & Other Creatures,* short stories, and *Skins,* a novel. *Skins* was produced as a feature film with a theatrical release in 2002. Louis has won various writing awards including Pushcart Prizes and fellowships from the Bush Foundation, the National Endowment for the Arts, and the Lila Wallace-Reader's Digest Foundation. His 2006 collection of poems, *Logorrhea* (Northwestern University Press), was a finalist for the Los Angeles Times Book Prize.